Contents

I am a nurse

My name is Kate. I am a nurse.

This is the hospital where I work.
It is called The County Hospital
and is in Hereford.

I am a children's nurse. There are twenty beds on the children's ward, and we usually have about ten **patients** at any one time.

The children's ward

Today I am on a day **shift**. I let myself in to the Children's Ward.

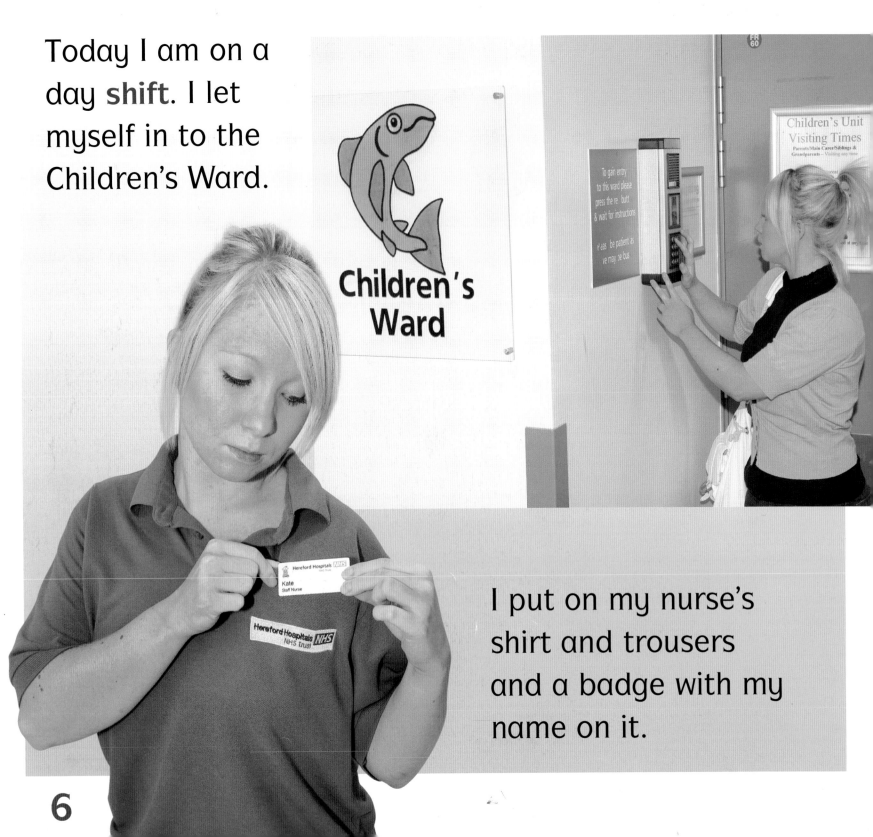

Children's
Ward

I put on my nurse's shirt and trousers and a badge with my name on it.

The night shift team will be going home soon.
I have a quick meeting with them and Clare
gives me the hand-over reports. These tell me
which children are on the ward, and who will
be joining us today.

Breakfast

This is Charlotte. She has just found out she has **diabetes**. She will be in the hospital for the day while the doctors do some tests.

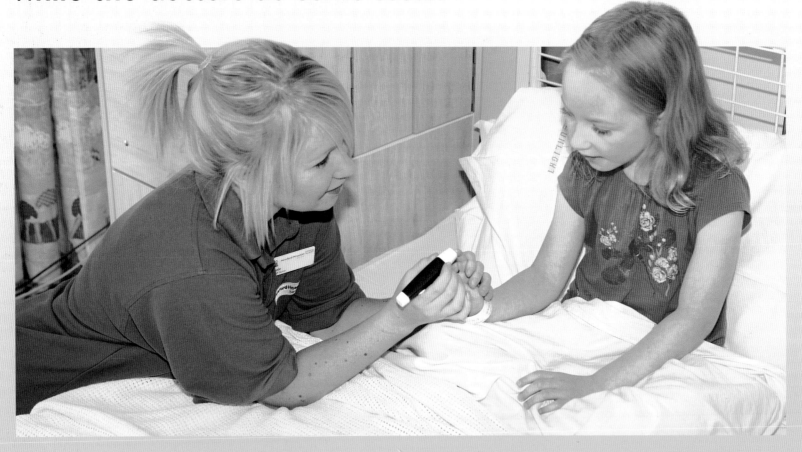

Charlotte needs a blood test. I take a tiny drop of blood with a special needle. It will be tested to see what her blood **glucose** level is.

I give Charlotte her breakfast and ask her what she would like for lunch.

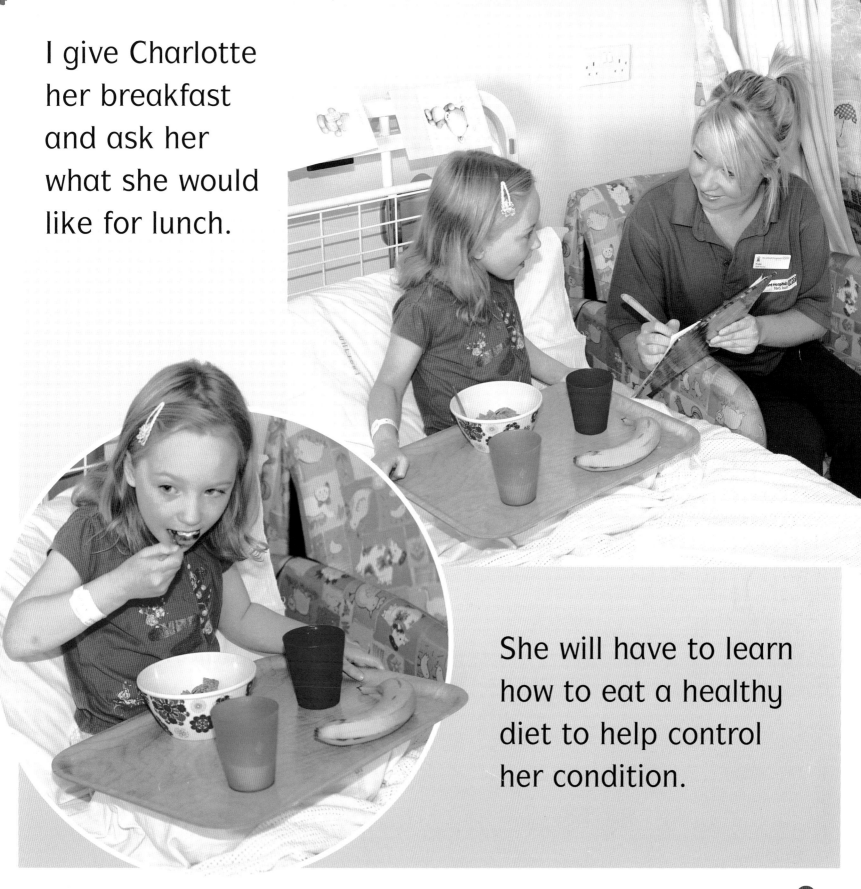

She will have to learn how to eat a healthy diet to help control her condition.

A new patient

Madeleine has arrived on the ward. Her dad has brought her in. She keeps getting **tonsillitis** and needs an operation to have her **tonsils** out.

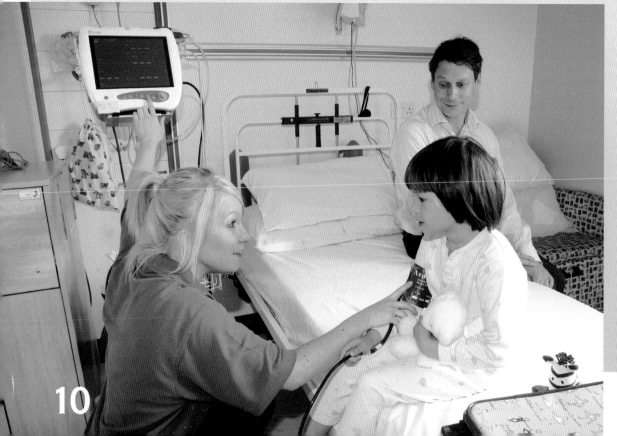

She puts her pyjamas on, and I take her **blood pressure**.

Then I weigh her on this weighing chair.
She weighs 18kg.

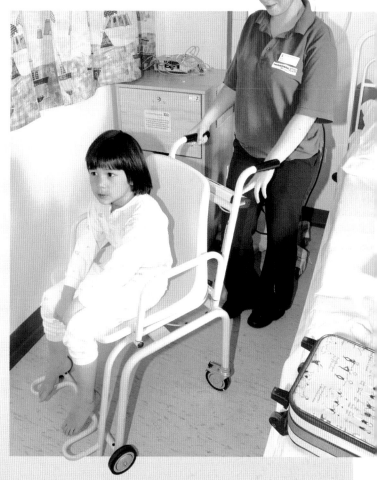

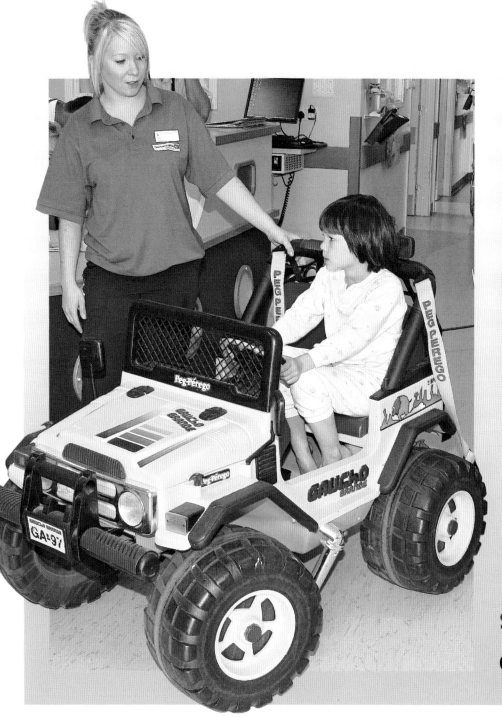

We have a special electric car for children who are going down to the **theatre** for **surgery**. Madeleine enjoys driving the car.

Ward round

Doctor Saleem has arrived to do the **ward round**.
He will check up on all the children in the ward.

Matthew broke his legs in a car accident. Doctor Saleem looks at Matthew's notes and asks how he is feeling. Matthew will need some **physiotherapy** to help his legs get strong again.

Then the doctor sees Charlotte. He shows her an **insulin pen**. She will have to carry one around with her. The **insulin** will control her diabetes.

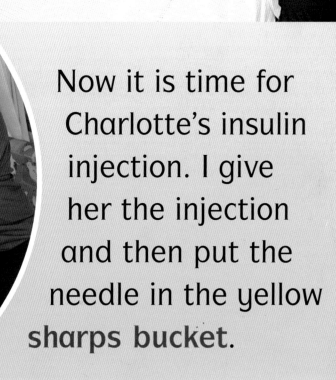

Now it is time for Charlotte's insulin injection. I give her the injection and then put the needle in the yellow **sharps bucket**.

Lunchtime

The lunch trolley has arrived on the ward.

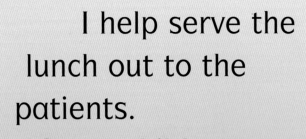

I help serve the lunch out to the patients.

Some children have lunch in bed, but Harry has his at the table.

14

Today I am meeting Jane for lunch. We choose some sandwiches at the hospital canteen.

Jane works in the Special Care Baby Unit. She looks after very small or **premature** babies. They are kept warm in **incubators**.

Playtime

Most children can get out of bed sometimes.
We have two playrooms for them to play in.

Harry challenges me to a game of pool. I expect
he will win as I am not very good.

Harry has an illness which means he has to visit us regularly. We look at a medical information book together and discuss his condition.

Next I play with Cosmo in the outdoor play area.

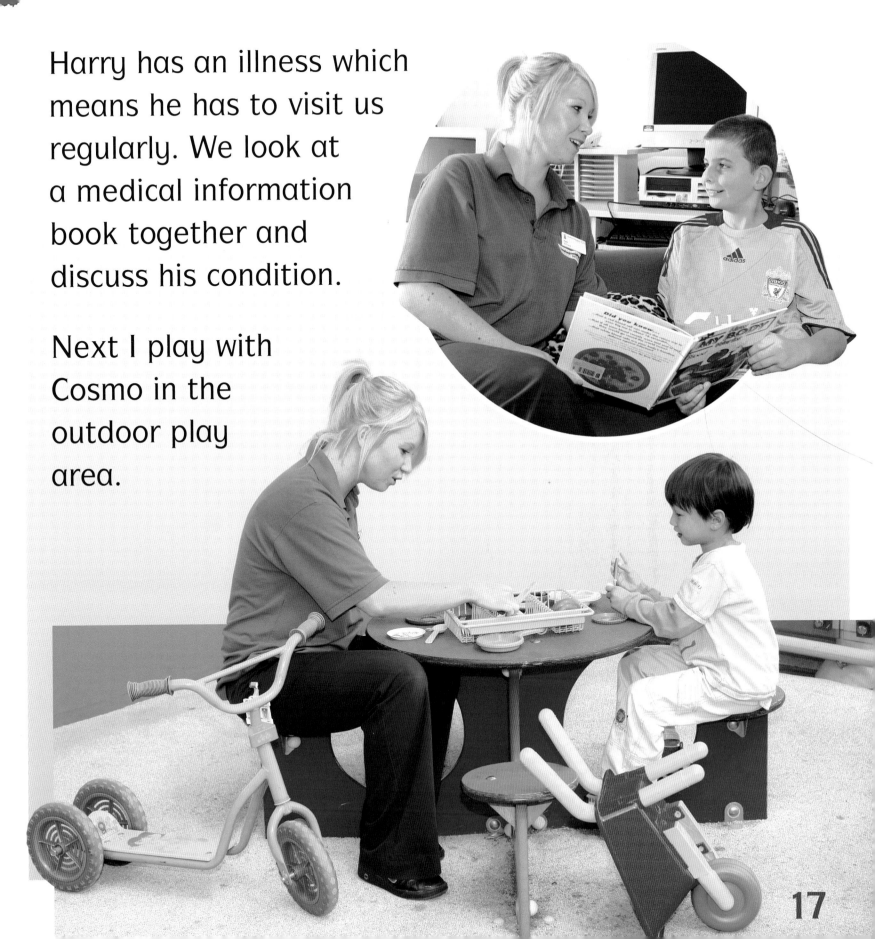

17

Back from theatre

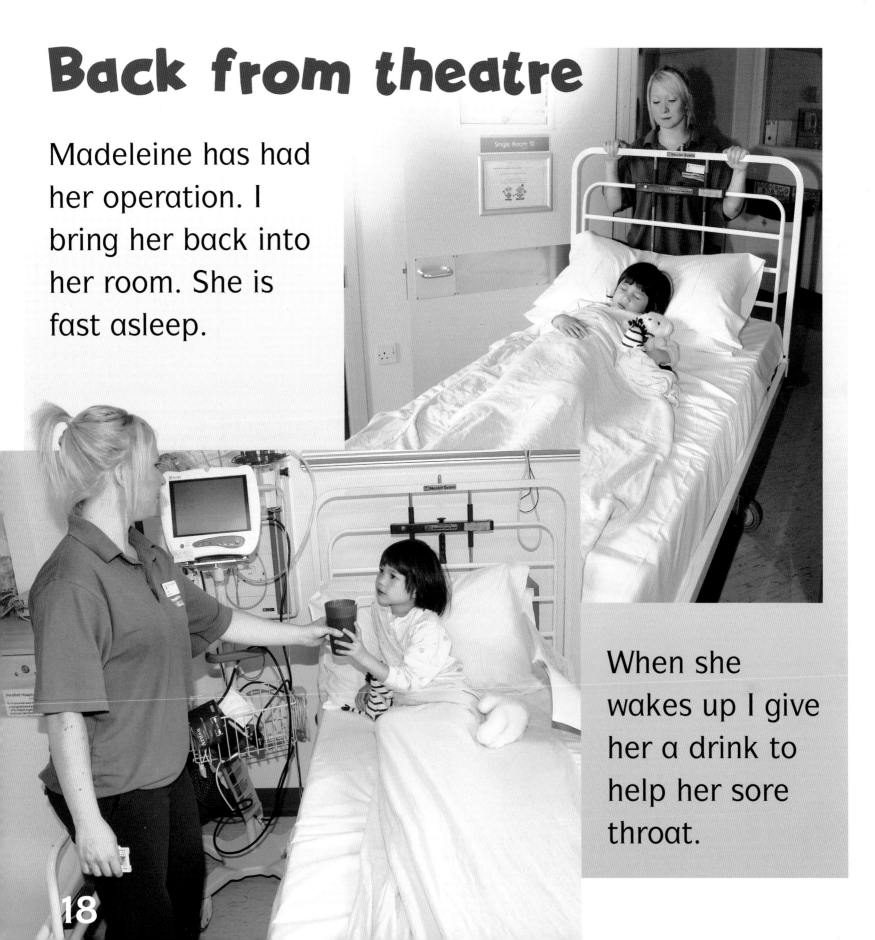

Madeleine has had her operation. I bring her back into her room. She is fast asleep.

When she wakes up I give her a drink to help her sore throat.

I take her
temperature.
The electronic
thermometer
says 36°C so
Madeleine's
temperature
is normal.

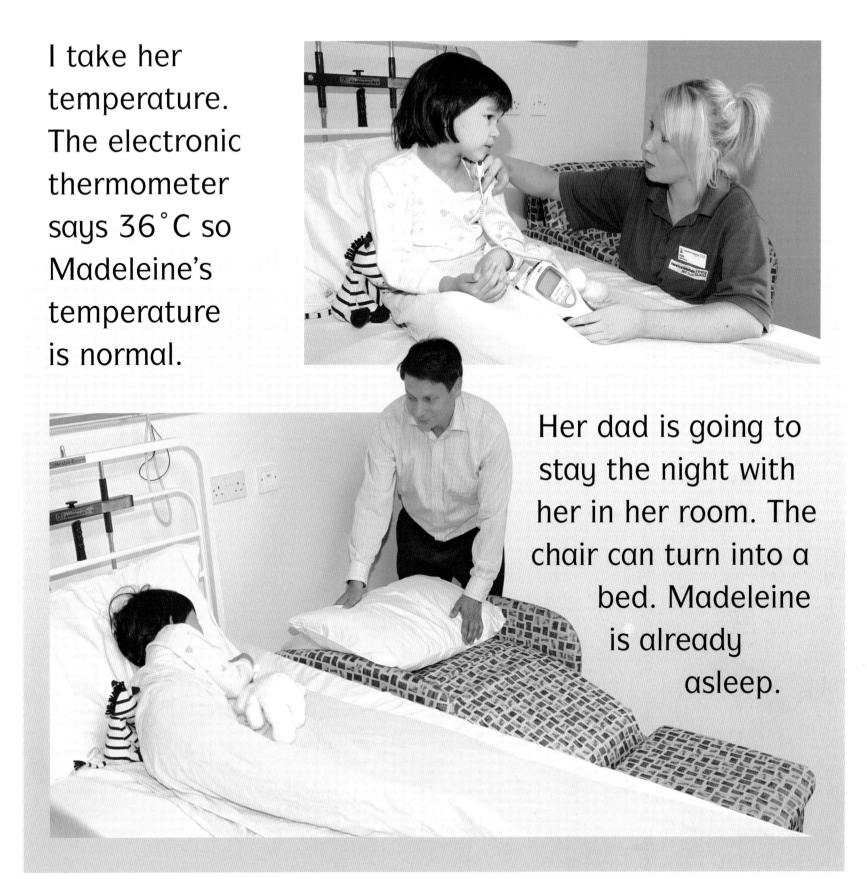

Her dad is going to
stay the night with
her in her room. The
chair can turn into a
bed. Madeleine
is already
asleep.

Updating records

It has been a busy day and it is nearly the end of my shift. I go to the staff kitchen and make myself a cup of tea.

Then I go back to the **reception** desk. I need to use the computer.

All the information about the patients is on the computer. I fill in the details of how all the patients are and what treatments they have had today. It is important to update the records often.

End of shift

It is now time for me to go home. Before I go, I give the hand-over reports to Ainsley. He is doing a **double shift**.

It has been a good day on the ward. I love being a nurse and helping sick children get better.

Glossary

blood pressure a measurement of how well your blood is pumping around your body

diabetes an illness where the body does not produce enough insulin, making people tired and thirsty

double shift doing two shifts of work, one after the other

glucose a type of sugar in the body

incubator a plastic cot in a hospital that keeps small babies warm and safe

insulin a hormone that controls the level of glucose in your blood

insulin pen a small machine that injects you with insulin

patients people who need to receive treatment from a doctor in a hospital

physiotherapy treating injuries by massaging and exercising the body

premature describes a baby that is born too early

reception the area in a hospital where patients and visitors are welcomed

sharps bucket a bucket where all used sharp objects like needles are put to be destroyed later

shift a part of the day that people take it in turns to work

surgery the process of operating on somebody

theatre the room in a hospital where operations happen

tonsillitis a disease of the tonsils

tonsils two small lumps of tissue at the back of the throat

ward round when a doctor visits all the patients on a ward to see how they are

Index